Looking at Transportation

D1651797

Looking at Passenger Aircraft

Cliff Lines

The Bookwright Press
New York · 1985

Looking at Transportation

Looking at Cars
Looking at Submarines
Looking at Trucks
Looking at Motorcycles
Looking at Passenger Aircraft

*This book is based on an
original text by G. A. Embleton*

First published in the United States in 1985 by
The Bookwright Press, 387 Park Avenue South,
New York, NY 10016
First published in 1984 by
Wayland (Publishers) Ltd
49 Lansdowne Place, Hove
East Sussex BN3 1HF, England

ISBN 0–531–03811–4
Library of Congress Catalog Card Number: 84–72074

Phototypeset by Kalligraphics Ltd, Redhill, Surrey
Printed in Italy by G. Canale & C.S.p.A., Turin

Contents

The first aircraft

Today we often see planes flying overhead.
We take them for granted and
forget that many of our grandparents were born before
the first plane ever flew.

This is Concorde which travels faster than sound.

Here is one of the first planes.
A few years earlier there were no planes at all.
The plane was piloted by Wilbur Wright, in 1909.
In 1903, Wilbur and his brother Orville had made
the first flight in a plane fitted with an engine.
They called their plane "Flyer I."

World War I began in 1914.
By that time planes could fly more than
160 km (100 miles) without landing.
Seaplanes had taken off and landed on water and
the first jumps had been made by parachute.

This is a World War I Handley Page bomber.

Here is a passenger climbing aboard
an early German plane.
He had to wear thick clothing to
keep warm in the open cockpit.

Flying was still a risky and costly business.
The planes were tiny and flimsily built.
They were made of wood and canvas and
used gasoline engines.
The pilots often had to land to make repairs.

This is a British de Havilland 4A used as
a bomber in World War I.

World War I lasted from 1914 to 1918.
During that time planes changed a great deal and
were used for many different jobs.
At first aircraft were only used to
see what the enemy was doing.
Then pilots began shooting at one another with
pistols and shotguns.
Soon planes were fitted with machine guns, and
the skies were filled with planes trying to
shoot each other down.
By 1918 planes were being used to bomb troops, and
German planes even bombed British towns.

Many war planes were sold off cheaply after the war.
They were used to start passenger services.
These passengers are on a French plane which flew
from Paris to London in under three hours in 1919.

There was not much room for passengers on
these early aircraft.
Flying was not a popular way of traveling because
only very rich people could afford the high fares, and
traveling by air was often cold and uncomfortable.

There were strict weight limits in those days and
every passenger had to be weighed to
make sure that the plane was not overloaded.

This German-made seaplane was used by
the Brazilian airline which started in 1927.

In the 1920s airlines began carrying mailbags.
There was more profit from a mailbag than from
a person of the same weight so passengers sometimes
had to sit among the sacks of letters.
Countries in Western Europe that ruled colonies
overseas started air services to these places.
British airlines flew passengers to colonies in Africa,
India and the Far East.
These long distances had to be covered in short hops
because the aircraft had to stop often to refuel.
There were no passenger flights in the United States
until the mid-1920s.

Services for the rich

By the 1930s there were regular passenger services but still only wealthy people could afford to use them.

Travel aboard these planes was very luxurious. Passengers sat in a cabin that looked like a first-class railroad car.

In 1935 this flying boat made the first airmail flight
across the Pacific from San Francisco to Manila.
With overnight stops it took six days.

Flying boats carried passengers on long trips.
Inside, these planes were decorated like
very fashionable restaurants.
When the planes stopped to refuel the
passengers stayed in hotels and went sightseeing.

This picture shows the airship Hindenburg
crashing at Lakehurst, N.J., in 1937.

Airships like the Hindenburg carried more than
50 passengers across the Atlantic in two days.
An airship was a huge wingless plane that
was filled with hydrogen.
The gondola where the passengers sat hung below
the airship and was very luxurious.
After the Hindenburg crash people were too nervous
to fly in airships again so the idea was dropped.
Some people are thinking of building them again
using a gas that does not burn.

Here is the dining room of a flying boat.

Here are some well-dressed passengers stepping
onto a Sikorsky flying boat.
Flying boats could land on the ground or on water.

During the 1920s and 1930s aircraft companies
started to make small planes
as well as big planes.

Small planes have made it possible to reach
places cut off from the rest of the world.
In Australia the Flying Doctor Service was started
in 1927 to answer urgent calls for help
from lonely cattle stations.
Many lives have been saved because
a plane can fly a sick person to a
distant hospital in two hours or less.

In 1931 this German plane was the biggest of its kind.
There were seats in the wings from which
passengers could look straight ahead.

Aircraft in wartime

During World War II, from 1939 to 1945,
huge numbers of aircraft were built to carry troops
and attack the enemy with bombs and bullets.
The war was fought in many parts of the world, and
aircraft were needed which could travel long
distances with heavy loads.

This British Avro Lancaster was built to fly
long distances.

These B17 Flying Fortresses were used by the
U.S. Air Force to bomb distant enemy targets.
They were well-armed with many
gun turrets as you can see.

Another American plane called the B24 Liberator
could fly across the Atlantic from Canada to
Britain on the fuel it could carry on board.

This Boeing 307 Stratoliner could fly
out of range of enemy fighters at
a height of 6,000 meters (20,000 ft).

Many improvements were made
to aircraft during the war.
Before the war all planes had propellers but
by 1945 some planes were powered by jet engines.
These sucked in air and heated and squeezed it before
pushing it out with such force that the plane was
driven forward at great speed.

Warplanes in peacetime

When the war ended in 1945, countries began to sell
hundreds of military aircraft they no longer needed.
To get rid of these aircraft quickly they were
sold at bargain prices.

These DC-3s were sold in England after 1945.
They were ideal for carrying passengers or goods.

Besides buying planes the civilian airlines used many runways that had been built in the war.

Here is a short runway in the hills of Indo-China.

This is the same runway before it was finished.

Many small airlines were started using these
wartime planes.
Thousands of people had worked with
aircraft during the war but
only a few of them were lucky enough to
find jobs with a civilian airline.

These British wartime Lancaster bombers were used to carry passengers after the war.

The new airlines and the airlines that had started before the war were kept very busy.

Abroad, many towns and factories were in ruins.
Countries had to start building up their trade again.
Companies that had made weapons, tanks and
warships had to find new goods to make and sell.
People flew around the world on business trips
and the airlines were kept busy.
Aircraft helped businesses to grow all over the world.
Few private passengers could afford the money
for air travel.

After the war, these American Flying Fortresses were
altered and renamed Stratocruisers and
used to carry passengers.

Aircraft were as useful in peacetime as
they had been during the war.
In 1949 the Russians stopped traffic along the
roads and railroads to West Berlin.
This part of the city was occupied by British,
American and French troops.
All supplies had to be flown in by air.
Civilian planes were called in to help the military.

This Boeing Stratocruiser was first used by Pan Am
for its service across the Atlantic in 1949.

These passengers are being served a meal on
a United Air Lines Stratocruiser in 1950.

The Stratocruiser carried 90 passengers in great luxury.
It had a bar on the lower deck which served drinks
and on the main deck there were beds which
could be folded away.

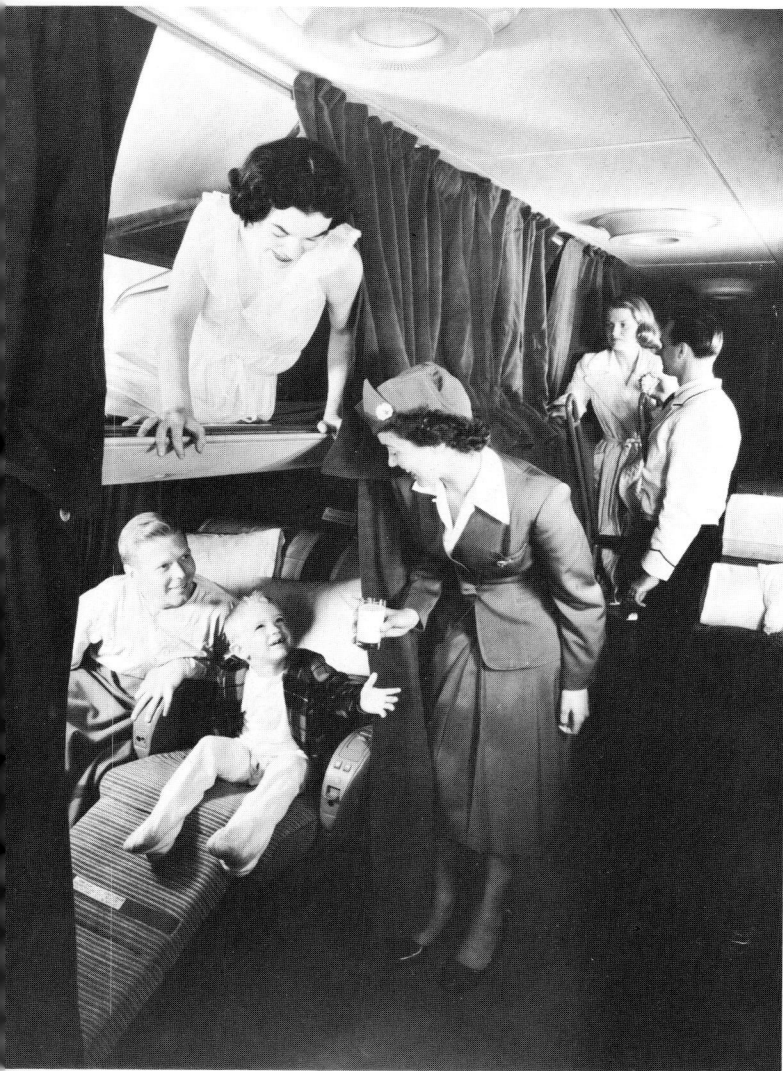

These are the sleeping berths on a Pan Am
Stratocruiser in the 1950s.
You could wake up to breakfast in bed at
a height of 7,500 m (25,000 ft) above sea level.

Planes for passengers

One of the first planes specially built to carry passengers was the Lockheed Constellation.

Here is the Lockheed Constellation which was first used by Pan American Airways in 1946.

High above the earth the air becomes very thin and
there is less oxygen to breathe.
Above 3,600 m (12,000 ft) oxygen masks must be worn
or the cabin must be made airtight so that
the air is kept in and
people can breathe normally.

This is the flight deck of a Constellation with
its crew of captain, copilot, radio operator and engineer.

This is a Lockheed Super Constellation.

Airtight cabins allow the passengers and crew to move about freely without wearing oxygen masks. If there is an accident and the cabin is no longer airtight, oxygen masks fall in front of the passengers so that they can breathe properly. It can be very dangerous for the passengers if something breaks through the wall of the airtight cabin when the plane is flying very high.

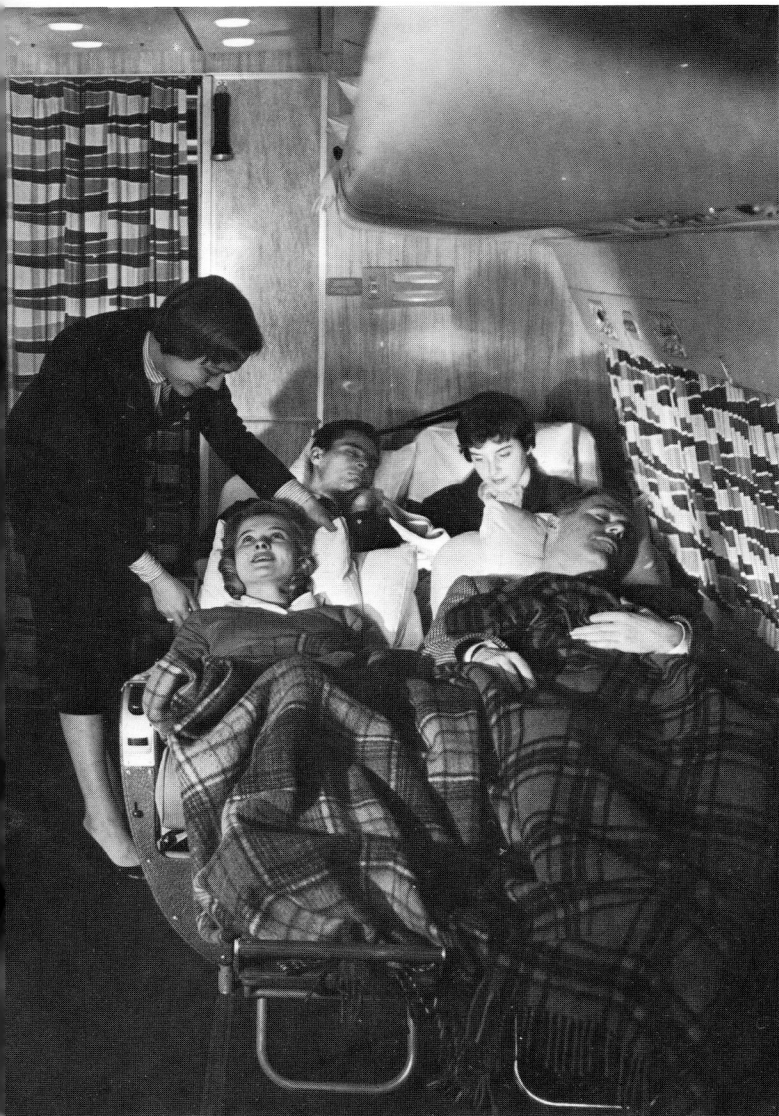

First-class passengers on a Constellation in 1958
enjoy the comfort of reclining seats.

▲

Planes like the Douglas DC-7C above and the
Boeing Strato Clipper below had airtight cabins.
They could fly above bad weather giving a
faster and more comfortable flight.

▼

Fast planes can fit in more trips than slow ones
and therefore carry more paying passengers.
Speed became very important and so
jet aircraft were introduced.
The first jet airliner was the BOAC de Havilland Comet
which flew from London to South Africa in 1952
with 35 passengers.
After several crashes most Comet jet airliners
were taken out of service.

These women are relaxing on a Pan Am Strato Clipper.

This is a more modern version of the Comet
which was known as the Comet 4B.

In the late 1950s a famous passenger jet called
the Boeing 707 began flying.
It became a very popular plane and was sold to
airlines all over the world.
It can cross the Atlantic at 960 km/h (600 mph)
in less than six hours carrying 190 passengers.

Why fly?

There are four main ways of moving people
and goods from place to place — by road, rail,
sea and air transportation.
Each method has its advantages and disadvantages.
Road traffic can go from door to door but
can only carry small loads.
Railroad trains can transport many more people and
goods but they cannot carry them from door to door.
The extra time and trouble taken in
getting to and from a railroad station makes
road transportation more attractive than
transportation by rail.
Many goods travel by sea.
Ships can carry more people and goods than
trains or road transportation.

Boeing 707 jets like this one are still being flown by
international airlines in many parts of the world.

This Qantas Boeing 747 "Jumbo" jet can fly from London to Sydney in 26 hours.
This includes a number of stops to refuel.

Ships have the disadvantage that they are slow and only carry their cargoes as far as the port.
This means that road or rail transportation must also be used to distribute the goods inland.
To save money and time ships have been designed so that cars and trucks can drive on and off quickly and easily.
Cargoes are sometimes packed in large containers that are easy to load and unload.
One advantage of sea transportation is that it is cheap.

Aircraft are expensive to run which makes
fares and cargo fees expensive.
Another disadvantage is that aircraft cannot
carry as many people or goods as ships.
But they reach their destinations very quickly and
the airports where they land are often within
easy reach of large towns.

These passengers are waiting in a crowded
airport lounge to board their plane.

Airports are kept busy night and day.
This is a Belgian plane at Kennedy Airport, New York,
which is one of the largest airports in the world.

Aircraft are also used to carry
valuable lightweight goods such as
cameras and expensive foods and flowers which
will only keep fresh for a short time.

Air travel becomes cheap

When your grandparents were young only a very few
rich people had been in an airplane.
If you have not already flown it is likely
that you will do so during your lifetime.
Millions of people fly each year and
in rich countries like the United States some people use
planes to fly to and from work each day.
Businesspeople living in London can fly to Rome
in the morning and be back in their office again
in the late afternoon.
It is even possible to fly from London to New York and
back in a day.
By leaving on the supersonic Concorde from London
at 10:30 a.m. you can be in New York by 9:25 a.m.
This is because the plane is so fast and there is a
five-hour time difference between the two cities.
A Concorde leaves New York in the early afternoon
and flies you to London at 11:25 p.m. the same day.
Of course a trip on Concorde is very expensive but
many people can afford to travel by slower aircraft.

Air travel has made the world seem a smaller place.
When your grandparents were young the only way
of getting to a distant place like Australia was by ship.
The journey took over six weeks and was very expensive.
Today many people can afford to fly that far
and it takes only a little over a day.

Passengers checking in at Heathrow Airport, London.
They will be given a seat number and
will have their luggage weighed to make sure
it is not too heavy.

These pictures show the differences between a plane cabin in the 1930s (top) and the first-class cabin of a modern Boeing 747 (bottom) which is nicknamed a Jumbo jet.

In 1976 Freddie Laker's "Skytrains," like this one, started
to fly passengers on the busy transatlantic route.
They charged less than $75 for a single ticket.
Although the company is no longer in operation,
transatlantic fares are still good value.

Fifty years ago most people went no farther
than the nearest beach resort for their vacations.
Many people now fly to other countries,
like Spain, Italy and Greece, for their vacations.
Travel agencies arrange tours that include
hotel costs as well as air fare.

Air travel today

A Jumbo jet is the largest passenger aircraft.
The tip of the tail is 19 m (63 ft) above the
ground and the wings have a span of 60 m (195 ft).
It weighs as much as 33 bull elephants.

Here you can see how big a Jumbo jet is
next to a Boeing 727.

This British Airways Jumbo carries 205,000 liters
(45,000 gallons) of fuel in its wings.
It can fly about 9,600 km (6,000 miles)
on this amount of fuel.
On each long flight the engines use up enough fuel
to fill a large swimming pool.
Four huge jet engines push the Jumbo through the
sky at more than 960 km/h (600 mph).

A Jumbo can carry well over 300 people and
their luggage for about 10 hours non-stop at
a height of 10 km (6 miles) above the earth.
The aircraft cost over $53 million each to buy.

The passengers sit in a comfortable cabin with
only the hum of the engines and sometimes
a sinking feeling to remind them they are flying.
The cabin has the same pressure as at ground level
and there are all sorts of things to
keep people from getting bored.
There are magazines to read, music to listen to
and movies to watch on long flights.
Cabin staff serve drinks and meals and
it is possible to stretch your legs by
walking in the aisles.

Here is a meal being served on a Boeing 747.

The airliner is full of complicated machinery and
is a maze of pipes and wiring.
All the power needed for the lights, air
conditioning and to cook the food is supplied
by one of the four engines.

This stewardess is preparing meals in
the galley of a Jumbo jet.
A large airline company has to prepare
enormous amounts of food because they often
carry more than 100,000 passengers a day.

Here are the pilot and his copilot operating
the controls on the flight deck.
The controls look very complicated with
hundreds of switches, dials and levers which
all have an important job to do.

The controls are linked to a computer so that
information can be fed to the automatic pilot.
Much of the time the plane is flown automatically.
If any instrument breaks down, a warning light
flashes and a spare instrument may take over.
A radio keeps the crew in touch with
the ground, and radar helps them to
keep on the right flight path.

This is a view of Amsterdam Airport from the air.
It is like a small town with its own roads,
shops, hospital, church, restaurants,
police force and fire service.
In a year more than 20 million passengers will
pass through here on their way to other places.

A large airline company may employ 50,000 people
and carry more than 100,000 passengers each day.

Growing larger

Before World War II started in 1939 the
airlines carried only a few passengers.
Because air fares were very high only the very
rich could afford to fly.
These people usually traveled in great luxury.

This Airbus A300 is the latest in a
long line of passenger aircraft.
It is built to carry a large number of passengers
in comfort but not in luxury.

Since World War II there has been
a huge increase in the number of air passengers.
Most working people now earn enough money
to take vacations abroad.
They do not want luxury travel but trips that
are fast, cheap and safe.
To meet this need the airlines ordered fleets of
jet airliners which could carry large numbers of
passengers without the frills of first-class travel.

This is the central computer used by the German
airline Lufthansa to look after its business.

As there are many more passengers the airlines have
been able to reduce the price of air fares.
Most international airlines belong to the IATA –
the International Air Transport Association – which
tries to make sure that there is
fair competition between airlines.

These passengers are checking in for a flight
at the airport in Düsseldorf, West Germany.

These passengers are going on a vacation trip arranged by a travel agency and British Airways.

Since the 1960s, business for the airlines and travel agents has gone up by leaps and bounds. The airlines are eager to fill every seat in their expensive jet planes otherwise they lose money. By working with the airlines, travel agencies have been able to offer very cheap "packaged" trips. The customer pays for a vacation which includes air travel, a hotel and sightseeing as part of the package.

Problems for the airlines

Many airlines get into financial difficulties because
planes are so expensive to run.
Some airlines are owned by the government of the
country where they are based.
If they lose money the governments will often
help them out with money raised from taxes.
As a result, these airlines may take on more and more
routes even though they cannot run them at a profit.

This is a British Airways Trident III
flying over central London.

One of the biggest expenses is fuel.
In 1973 the price of oil began to rise sharply and
the airlines had to pay much more for their fuel.
The airlines also found they had fewer passengers and
started a price war, cutting rates to encourage more
people to fly with them.

This is Kennedy Airport, New York's international
airport.

These tourists are about to board an aircraft in Nepal.
Nepal is a mountainous country few people had
visited before aircraft made it easy to reach.
The elephant is used as a taxi!

Airlines will continue to have difficulties because
there are too many aircraft operating on
too few routes and it is not always easy to
fill planes and make them pay.
Most airlines will survive but some may have to
cut back their services to stay in business.

The effects of air travel

Rich countries benefit most from air travel.
Flying helps businesses to expand and
improves communication which is
so important to modern-day life.
It also provides jobs for many people.

Helicopters are sometimes used to
ferry passengers over short distances.

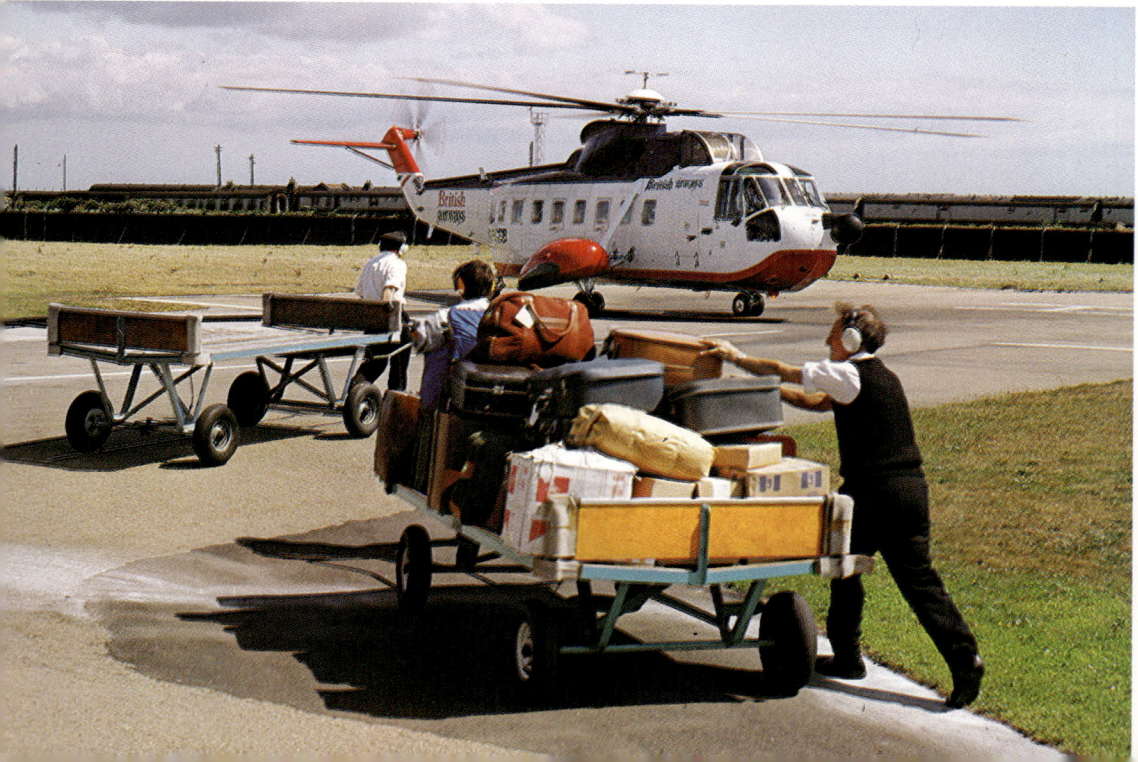

▲

Air travel can also help poorer countries.
This lonely spot in South Yemen is now
easier to reach because of air travel.

With the increase of passenger aircraft, many countries
are now less cut off from the rest of the world.
In times of famine, planes can quickly fly
supplies of food and
medicine to troubled areas.

Air travel has brought with it certain problems.
It has greatly increased the pace of life and
can lead to the quick spread of diseases.
It makes life noisy for those people who
live close to an international airport.
But the benefits of air travel are
greater than the drawbacks.

This Short's Skyvan is a British plane used to carry
passengers or goods over short distances.

Here is a British Airways supersonic Concorde
outside its hangar at Heathrow.

It is difficult for us to imagine what the
world would be like without passenger aircraft.
Fifty years ago there were hardly any planes at
all and people then could only guess at
the changes that were to come.
Perhaps in another 50 years there will
be fleets of spaceships to take us to other planets.

Glossary

Airship   An aircraft which is filled with gas
to make it float.
The airship is powered by engines and has
cabins for the passengers.

Airtight cabin   Jet aircraft fly at heights where
there is very little air so their cabins
are made strong and airtight.
They can then hold air at the same pressure
as it is on the ground.

Flight deck   The forward part of an aircraft
where the crew sit.

Flying boat   An airplane that can land on or take off
from water.

Hangar   A large building used for storing or
repairing aircraft.

Helicopter   An aircraft with horizontal
propellers which allow it to take off
and land on one spot.

Jumbo jet   The name given to very large passenger
planes such as the Boeing 747.

Radar   An instrument for measuring the distance
to an object by means of radio waves.
These are bounced off the object and
appear on a radar screen as dots of light.

Radio beacon   A fixed point on the ground which
sends out radio signals.
These are picked up by an airliner and used
to calculate the plane's position and route.

Runway   The part of an airfield used by planes for
landing and taking off.

Supersonic plane   A plane that travels faster than
sound. The Concorde is supersonic because it
travels at twice the speed of sound —
about 2,250 km/h (1,400 mph).

Index

Picture acknowledgments

The illustrations in this book were supplied by: Air France 9; Associated Press 15; Alan Beaumont 31; Brenard Photographic Services Ltd. *front cover*; British Aerospace 4; British Airways 8, 12, 18, 42, 46, 54, 55; Robert Hunt Library 6, 19, 20, 21, 24, 25; Lufthansa 7, 10, 11, 17, 22, 23, 32, 52; Pan Am 13, 14, 16, 26, 28, 29, 30, 33 (both), 34, 36, 45; Qantas 38, 47; Short Bros. 60; United Air Lines 27, 43; Wayland Picture Library 5; Zefa 35, 39, 40, 44, 48, 49, 50, 51, 53, 56, 57, 58, 59, 61.